Fifty Shades of Faith

By Stephanie Flores

Heart Thoughts Publishing
Floyds Knobs, IN

Unless otherwise indicated, the Scriptures quoted are taken from the New English Translation (NET) of the Bible.

NET Bible® copyright ©1996-2006 by Biblical Studies Press, L.L.C. http://netbible.com All rights reserved.

The names: THE NET BIBLE®, NEW ENGLISH TRANSLATION COPYRIGHT © 1996 BY BIBLICAL STUDIES PRESS, L.L.C. NET Bible® IS A REGISTERED TRADEMARK THE NET BIBLE® LOGO, SERVICE MARK COPYRIGHT © 1997 BY BIBLICAL STUDIES PRESS, L.L.C. ALL RIGHTS RESERVED

Printed in the United States of America

First Printing, 2015

ISBN-13:978-1517784843
ISBN-10:1517784840
LCCN: 2015955281

Heart Thoughts Publishing
P.O. Box 536
Floyds Knobs, IN 47119

Dedication

This book is dedicated to my husband, Mike, who has encouraged me to keep going and never give up. To my beautiful children, Tarrah (Rashid Hill), Brittany, Briona, Michaela, Mike Jr., Saige and Stephen; each one of you have blessed my life more than you will ever know. To my adorable grands, Talea, Talen, Tegan, Tianna and Brayden; you remind me daily how sweet the Love of Christ is. To the greatest parents on earth, Morgan and Charlotte Hearn who made me go to church and have been an example of what it means to love unconditionally. To my siblings; Richard, Robert, Michael, Pamela, Sheila, Kimberly and Monica; without you I wouldn't know what it is like to be a friend or to have a friend because you all were my first best friends.

To all my family and friends, Second Baptist Church of New Albany, Indiana, Commitment Community Church family of Lindenwold New Jersey, Northside Christian Church family of New Albany, Indiana, Liberty Church of Louisville, Kentucky and First Baptist Church family of Warrensburg, Missouri.

To Vanessa Collins of Heart Thoughts Publishing; you believed and supported me at times when I didn't believe in myself.

Most of all, I want to thank my GREAT and Mighty God. Without Him, I am and can do nothing!

Table of Contents

Introduction

In life there are times of great joy and great sorrow. Anyone can love God in the good, in the sunshine. But even in the sunshine things can get too hot and we at times seek comfort in the cool of the shade. When the heat of this life gets turned up, do you trust Him to give you relief?

As you read each "shade of faith," know that He is always there watching over you, calling you into the shade: His shadow of comfort over your life.

Shade 1

Most Christians have been walking with the Lord for years but have never bowed down before Him. We have never submitted our hearts, tongues, attitudes and actions fully to Him. Sometimes we "seasoned" Christians forget that we are still a work in progress. Psalm 95:6 says:

> *Come! Let's bow down and worship! Let's kneel before the LORD, our creator!*

Let's come down off our high seats and bow down before Him. Today, take a moment to bow down. Bring your flesh down. What a great reward to kiss His feet! He desires and is waiting on you.

Blessings! ☺

Meditate on Psalm 95:6 today. Write in your Faith Journal what you experienced from bowing down before Him.

Shade 2

Yep! He Loves Me.

Our souls are God's treasure and Satan wants to steal it away. Our soul has an enemy and we are in a very real battle. Our God, in His great love for us, has given us His Word that it may be our defense. It is sharper than any two edged sword. It will cut through the darkest parts of our lives and carve the way to His brilliant light. He longs for you to know His heart and it rapidly beats for you. The only way to know Him is through His Word. Make an appointment with Him. He has so much to tell you.

Meditate on Hebrews 4:12:

> For the word of God is living and active and sharper than any double-edged sword, piercing even to the point of dividing soul from spirit, and joints from marrow; it is able to judge the desires and thoughts of the heart.

Write in your Faith Journal what new things were revealed about God in your "appointment" with Him.

Shade 3

We are all a "hot mess" in need of His Message. Don't be so holy that your heart is as a diamond: really shiny and pretty but unable to be pierced by another's struggle. If Christ left His throne in Heaven to save us, we can surely leave our comforts to bring life to others. All of us are in need of a Savior. Are you willing to be His light so that the lost may be found?

Blessings! ☺

Meditate on Isaiah 65:5:

> They say, 'Keep to yourself! Don't get near me, for I am holier than you!' These people are like smoke in my nostrils, like a fire that keeps burning all day long.

Write in your Faith Journal how you may have an attitude of "holier than thou" and how you plan to change it.

Shade 4

If believers would try to love others right where they are, imagine how much HOPE we'd have in the future. We are all broken and fractured in some way but Healed by His blood. See others with His eyes as beautiful creations; unique and priceless, fragile yet strong. Each one, crazy loved, by God.

Blessings,

Meditate on Proverbs 25:21-22:
> If your enemy is hungry, give him food to eat, and if he is thirsty, give him water to drink, for you will heap coals of fire on his head, and the Lord will reward you.

Write in your Faith Journal ways you can be the Love and Light of Christ to others.

Shade 5

Yep...He Loves Me

Jesus...just the whisper of His name brings hope. He will invade your heart like rushing water. Oh how sweet the taste of His love. With one glimpse of Him, your life is made new. One moment in His presence, you'll find the peace of a lifetime. I'm in awe that Jesus, in all His perfection, "crazy loves" such imperfect people...but he does. He is steadfast. Yes...Jesus Loves me...and He loves You!

Blessings,

Meditate on Romans 5:8:
> *But God demonstrates his own love for us, in that while we were still sinners, Christ died for us.*

Write in your Faith Journal some of the ways you have felt His love today.

Shade 6

Yep...He loves me.

I'm so glad our God is the same yesterday, today, tomorrow and forever. We never have to wonder if He loves us. His love is everlasting.

Blessings,

Meditate on this scripture: Hebrews 13:8:
> *Jesus Christ is the same yesterday and today and forever!*

Write in your Faith Journal what knowing this truth means to you

Shade 7

Yep...HE loves me.

Who is like the Lord, our God? His love gave us breath and is so overwhelming it takes our breath away. He takes our mess and covers it with hope. He loves us just that much. There is no one like our God.

Blessings ☺

Meditate on Ephesians 2:4-5:
> *But God, being rich in mercy, because of his great love with which he loved us, even though we were dead in transgressions, made us alive together with Christ—by grace you are saved!*

Write in your Faith Journal how this will help you in your walk with Christ.

Shade 8

Yep...He loves me.

You have called me yours. Lord, I hear your voice as I meditate on Your Word. You refresh my heart. Your breath is fresh air to my lungs. I am revived in You. You love me unconditionally. Yes...You are mine and I am yours. I will worship You forever.

Blessings,

Meditate on Song of Solomon 2:16:
> *My lover is mine and I am his; he grazes among the lilies.*

Write in your Faith Journal what it means to belong to Him.

Shade 9

Check yourself before you wreck yourself!

Sometimes we need to take a pause and realize we have been trudging down the wrong path. If your spirit is in a state of constant struggle, you may need a pause to clear out the fog so that you can see the road God has already cleared for you. In our struggles, if we are in Christ, we can still have peace. But, if you are in a struggle and there is no peace; pause, listen and obey! He is holding the detour sign in His hands and will lead you back on the right path.

Blessings! ☺

Meditate on 1 Corinthians 14:33:
> *For God is not characterized by disorder but by peace. As in all the churches of the saints,*

Write in your Faith Journal how meditating on this scripture helped you throughout your day.

Shade 10

Every time we use the gift of speech to tear down, gossip, and lie we've just signed up as a volunteer for the devil. There is life and death in the tongue. Jesus promises life. Satan seeks your death. Don't give in that easily. If we belong to Christ, we are in the Army of The Lord! Encourage, empower, and love each other. The world will never want what we say we have if our tongues are laced with maggots. Ugh...be life!

Blessings! ☺

Meditate on Proverbs 18:21:
> Death and life are in the power of the tongue,
> and those who love its use will eat its fruit.

Write in your Faith Journal how this scripture has challenged you to become aware of your words.

Shade 11

Yep...He loves me.

The fact that He chose me to choose Him is something my small mind cannot fully understand. But I know He loves me. He left heaven to rescue me from myself. Such love is too wonderful for me. Oh how He must love us!

Meditate on Ephesians 1:4:

For he chose us in Christ before the foundation of the world that we may be holy and unblemished in his sight in love.

Write in your Faith Journal what the word "chosen" means to you in light of this scripture.

Shade 12

YOU are special! Stop allowing the world define you. You are created in His image. Why do you look at yourself and wish you were different or looked different? YOU are a child of the One True King! He has carved you out with His very own hands and with a very unique plan only for you. You are one of a kind! Step out and trust Him!

Blessings! ☺

Meditate on Psalm 139:14 (NIV)

I praise you because I am fearfully and wonderfully made; your works are wonderful, I know that full well.

Write in your Faith Journal what this scripture has meant to you today.

Shade 13

Do you realize that the greatest gift you will ever have is the knowledge of the Love of Christ. No matter what this world will ever say or think about you, to Him you are precious and priceless.

Meditate on Ephesians 3:17-18
> *So that Christ may dwell in your hearts through faith. And I pray that you, being rooted and established in love, may have power, together with all the Lord's holy people, to grasp how wide and long and high and deep is the love of Christ.*

Write in your Faith Journal what this scripture has spoken to your heart today.

Shade 14

Stop Running!

We all get tired of the craziness of life. Yet we keep trying to run our lives and everyone else's life. Most of us are running from the very thing that will give us rest. Seek His face. If you're going to run, run into His arms. He will give you rest. Take off those "runnin' it" shoes and walk in His sandals.

Blessings! ☺

Meditate on Isaiah 48:17 (NIV)
> *This is what the LORD says-- your Redeemer, the Holy One of Israel: "I am the LORD your God, who teaches you what is best for you, who directs you in the way you should go.*

Write in Your Faith Journal how you can let go and let God.

Shade 15

No matter if you're running or sitting still, God is relentless in His pursuit of you. He knocks at the door constantly until you acknowledge Him freely or until you have no choice but to bow before Him. His plan for your life wasn't meant to be lived without Him. He longs to dwell with you. STOP running. STOP ignoring. Answer the door...let Him in, not as a guest on the weekends but as the Lord of your everyday life.

Blessings,

Meditate on Revelation 3:20

> *Listen! I am standing at the door and knocking! If anyone hears my voice and opens the door I will come into his home and share a meal with him, and he with me.*

Romans 14:11

> *For it is written, "As I live, says the Lord, every knee will bow to me, and every tongue will give praise to God."*

Shade 16

No One is greater than our God. No situation is bigger than our God. He seeks hearts wide open to Him, knees bowed only to Him and hands outstretched to Him. He is right in the middle of it all. He IS the center of all...holding all things in place. Storms will come and the clouds will move but in His strength you will stand. Our God is greater.

Blessings,

Meditate on 1 John 4:4

> *You are from God, little children, and have conquered them, because the one who is in you is greater than the one who is in the world.*

Write in your Faith Journal about a time when God revealed Himself great in a situation in your life. He is still that same God.

Shade 17

LIVE a life worthy of your Calling.

LAUGH in the face of negativity and keep living.

LOVE one another DEEPLY!

LIVE-LAUGH-LOVE....I dare ya!

Meditate on Ephesians 4:1-16

I, therefore, the prisoner for the Lord, urge you to live worthily of the calling with which you have been called, with all humility and gentleness, with patience, bearing with one another in love, making every effort to keep the unity of the Spirit in the bond of peace. There is one body and one Spirit, just as you too were called to the one hope of your calling, one Lord, one faith, one baptism, one God and Father of all, who is over all and through all and in all. But to each one of us grace was given according to the measure of the gift of Christ. Therefore it says, "When he ascended on high he captured captives; he gave gifts to men." Now what is the meaning of "he ascended," except that he also descended to the lower regions, namely, the earth? He, the very one who descended, is also the one who ascended above all the heavens, in order to fill all things. It was he who gave some as apostles, some as prophets, some as evangelists, and some as pastors and teachers, to equip the saints for the work of ministry, that is, to build up the body of Christ, until we all attain to the unity of the faith and of the knowledge of the Son of God—a mature person, attaining to the measure of Christ's full stature. So we are no longer to be children, tossed back and forth by waves and carried about by every wind of teaching by the trickery of people who craftily carry out their deceitful schemes. But practicing the truth in love, we will in all things grow up into Christ, who is the head. From him the whole body grows, fitted and held together through every supporting ligament. As each one does its part, the body grows in love.

Write in your Faith Journal how you plan to be active in a love that seeks the best for others.

Shade 18

My parents used to say you can kill a bee with honey every time. I believe you can win hearts for Christ with LOVE...not condemnation. If you want to see real change...LOVE OTHERS. Christ changed this whole world by His LOVE. So...grab some honey and a couple of biscuits and love on someone today. By the way...watch out for bees.

Blessings! ☺

Meditate on Proverbs 16:24
> *Pleasant words are like a honeycomb, sweet to the soul and healing to the bones.*

Write in your Faith Journal how a sweet word of encouragement helped you in the past.

Shade 19

Hope knows the mystery of the future. Hope will keep you pressing toward it. Make sure your hope is anchored in Christ. Your future will be no mystery.

Blessings! ☺

Meditate on Colossians 1:27

> *God wanted to make known to them the glorious riches of this mystery among the Gentiles, which is Christ in you, the hope of glory.*

Write in your Faith Journal how it feels to know that you will be with Christ forever.

Shade 20

Your faith will open doors your life has slammed shut! When you BELIEVE His Word, He will take what's impossible and make it reality! He will take what's tarnished and make it shine. Get into God's Word. Get God's Word into You! His plan for your life is AMAZING!

Meditate on Matthew 17:20:

> *He told them, "It was because of your little faith. I tell you the truth, if you have faith the size of a mustard seed, you will say to this mountain, 'Move from here to there,' and it will move; nothing will be impossible for you."*

Write in your Faith Journal a time when you thought a situation was impossible and God made it possible. Looking back now, should you doubt Him?

Shade 21

There is no place I can go that God is not with me. In my sorrow, joy, day or night, my comings and goings, HE is there. He was with me before I was born, watching over His creation, imparting the fruit of the Spirit...love, joy, peace, long-suffering, kindness, goodness, faithfulness, gentleness and self-control into my marrow, that I may be found in HIM. I am never alone for He is woven within me.

Meditate on Galatians 5:22
> *But the fruit of the Spirit is love, joy, peace, patience, kindness, goodness, faithfulness,*

Jeremiah 1:5
> *Before I formed you in your mother's womb I chose you. Before you were born I set you apart. I appointed you to be a prophet to the nations.*

Write in your Faith Journal how you feel knowing HE had a plan for your life and watches over you and that plan which He placed in you since the beginning of time.

Shade 22

Are there things or relationships in your life that you haven't reconciled yet? It is not too late. TODAY is the day. Jesus is all about making the wrongs right and the old new. He wants you to live at peace and in peace with others. That requires you having the Peace of Christ. Pray. Spend time alone with Him. He will lead you to the reconciliation of all things. He is the way. HE makes all things new.

Meditate on 2 Corinthians 5:17
> So then, if anyone is in Christ, he is a new creation; what is old has passed away—look, what is new has come!

Write in your Faith Journal some things that you have not reconciled. Pray over them. Do not allow them room any longer. If you need to forgive or be forgiven, settle it today and now that God makes it all new and you no longer have to live in the bondage of the old.

Shade 23

All hell may be swirling around you but it can NEVER overtake you. You may have taken a few hits to the chin and the enemy may think he has backed you into a corner. But the moment you call on JESUS, hell has to take a knee and get back under the earth. You will not be defeated!

Blessings! ☺

Meditate on Romans 10:13:

> *For everyone who calls on the name of the Lord will be saved.*

Write in your Faith Journal someone you know that has not accepted the free gift of Salvation and commit to praying for them and being the light in this dark world that leads them to His Grace.

Shade 24

Being religious is no way to live. Live according to the Christ in you. Allow Him to reign in your life, to guide your every step. Allow HIM access and HE will change how you, think, speak, act and give you a joy you can't contain. There is a better way to live...in relationship with Christ.

Blessings! ☺

Meditate on Psalm 1:1-3:

> *How blessed is the one who does not follow the advice of the wicked, or stand in the pathway with sinners, or sit in the assembly of scoffers! Instead he finds pleasure in obeying the Lord's commands; he meditates on his commands day and night. He is like a tree planted by flowing streams; it yields its fruit at the proper time, and its leaves never fall off. He succeeds in everything he attempts.*

Write in your Faith Journal a time when you were "religious" in thinking and how it affected your life. Then write about a time when you were living in "relationship" with Christ and how it affected you.

Shade 25

When the mess of your past comes knocking at the door, wanting to pull you back and invade the space you are in now...DO NOT OPEN THE DOOR! It's the messenger of old news and GOD is doing a new thing in and through your life. Keep moving forward!

Blessings! ☺

Meditate on Isaiah 43:18-19:
> Don't remember these earlier events; don't recall these former events. Look, I am about to do something new. Now it begins to happen! Do you not recognize it? Yes, I will make a road in the desert and paths in the wilderness.

Write in your Faith Journal ways you can move forward and stop answering the door to the past.

Shade 26

My dad once told me that most of the people who praise you will be the first to say "off with your head." Let everything you do be for the glory of God so that when they come for you with the hatchet, The Armor of the Lord covers you.

A lot of times we are so eager to please people. It was placed in us from the beginning to desire love, acceptance and fellowship. But when we place others before God, we are setting ourselves up to be wounded. People will fail you but GOD never will.

Meditate on Psalm 136:26:
> *Give thanks to the God of heaven, for his loyal love endures!*

Write in your Faith Journal some of the names of God and spend time worshipping Him, thanking Him, giving honor to only Him.

Shade 27

I have come to know that when you trust HIM with all your heart, NOTHING and NO ONE can stop you! Jesus has a plan for you. Your very steps have carefully and lovingly been mapped out. Walk in faith. Go ahead; take that first step, even if you have to tip toe...HE'S GOT YOU!

Meditate on Jeremiah 29:11:
> *For I know what I have planned for you,' says the Lord. 'I have plans to prosper you, not to harm you. I have plans to give you a future filled with hope.*

Write in your Faith Journal something you know God has called you to do but you have been afraid or you have put it off. Then make an action plan to get it done, knowing He has already given you the tools to succeed.

Shade 28

I hear the chains falling! The bondage of addictions, alcoholism, low self-esteem, poverty, joblessness, slander, divorce, loneliness, sexual abuse, psychological issues, relationships...whatever has you bound MUST let you go. There is power in the name of Jesus to break EVERY chain! Believe it. Call on Him. You have already been set free!

Meditate on Hebrews 1:3-4:

> *The Son is the radiance of his glory and the representation of his essence, and he sustains all things by his powerful word, and so when he had accomplished cleansing for sins, he sat down at the right hand of the Majesty on high. Thus he became so far better than the angels as he has inherited a name superior to theirs.*

Write in your Faith Journal how you ARE going to trust God with the situations in your life and become free of the chains as you link your heart and hope to Christ who is seated at the right hand of God.

Shade 29

Finally, brothers and sisters, whatever is true, whatever is worthy of respect, whatever is just, whatever is pure, whatever is lovely, whatever is commendable, if something is excellent or praiseworthy, think about these things.

Philippians 4:8

God did not ASK you to think on these things, He commanded it! When your mind is crowded with all things opposite of what He Himself has commanded, You are disobedient! God knows how those things will keep you from Him. We are always saying, "I just want to be Happy." Well, He has given you the key to having an abundant life and everlasting joy. It starts in your mind. What are you thinking? What you think in your mind will establish roots in your heart. Your heart is the way of your life. He has given you 7 things to think about over the course of a 7 day week. Pick one a day and keep Him close always.

Blessings! ☺

Write in your Faith Journal some of the good, pure, lovely, true, just, virtuous and praiseworthy things in your life.

Shade 30

Knowing Him brings new life and greater hope. You begin to know who you are in Him. Know that you are of value. Know that you are of worth. Know that you are the apple of His eye. Know that your future days are better than your past. Know that YOU ARE LOVED COMPLETELY by Him. Breathe in His love. Exhale it onto others so that they may know Him and know new life!

Blessings! ☺

Meditate on 1 John 2:3-6

> Now by this we know that we have come to know God: if we keep his commandments. The one who says "I have come to know God" and yet does not keep his commandments is a liar, and the truth is not in such a person. But whoever obeys his word, truly in this person the love of God has been perfected. By this we know that we are in him. The one who says he resides in God ought himself to walk just as Jesus walked.

Write in your Faith Journal what you KNOW to be true about God and ways you can get to know Him better.

Shade 31

When your heart feels too heavy for your chest, worried with all the cares of this world...exchange all your cares for the cares of Christ. Trade your worry for His wonder, your trials for His truth, the lies for His love and that heaviness will become a hallelujah!

Praise + Prayer= Peace!

Meditate on 1 Peter 5:7:
> *And God will exalt you in due time, if you humble yourselves under his mighty hand by casting all your cares on him because he cares for you.*

Write in your Faith Journal how you will decide to turn all your concerns over to Him and leave them there.

Shade 32

I am so thankful to be able to see with my eyes shut, the Glory of God all around me. It is wonderful to hear Him call me without an audible voice and to feel His warm embrace without a physical touch. Thank you Holy Spirit...You are every beat of my heart.

Meditate on Romans 15:13:
> *Now may the God of hope fill you with all joy and peace as you believe in him, so that you*

may abound in hope by the power of the Holy Spirit.

Galatians 4:6

And because you are sons, God sent the Spirit of his Son into our hearts, who calls "Abba! Father!"

Write in your Faith Journal what it means to you to have "ABBA FATHER" as your guardian.

Shade 33

You are so faithful. You make the crooked straight, the weak strong, the hurting healed, the hated loved and the lost found.

Thank you, Jesus. You never leave...even when we are far away. So Grateful!

Meditate on 2 Thessalonians 3:3:
But the Lord is faithful, and he will strengthen you and protect you from the evil one.

Write in your Faith Journal how God was faithful, even when you were not so faithful.

Shade 34

Fear is NOT an excuse! It's a thief! It will steal your dreams, your future and your abundant life. You have authority over fear. Trust God. Choose to move forward. See that relationship, that ministry, that job, that business, that gift, that dream or that hope become a reality. Don't be frozen by fear. Get goosebumps from the excitement of your future.

Blessings! ☺

Say it with me: Fear won't freeze my future!

Meditate on Isaiah 41:10:

> *Don't be afraid, for I am with you! Don't be frightened, for I am your God! I strengthen you—yes, I help you—yes, I uphold you with my saving right hand!*

Write in your Faith Journal how you are going to overcome the fear in your life and get unstuck.

Shade 35

He will hear your cry. Sometimes our answer to prayer doesn't come in a pretty package wrapped in a bow. But I praise God because He heard me and that alone is a gift.

Blessings! ☺

Meditate on Isaiah 30:19

> For people will live in Zion; in Jerusalem you will weep no more. When he hears your cry of despair, he will indeed show you mercy; when he hears it, he will respond to you.

Write in your Prayer Journal an answer to prayer that was nothing like you expected.

Shade 36

He's always there!

Lord, I know you are there...hovering, patiently waiting. Lord, I bow down and worship You alone. I praise You because You are worthy to be praised. I seek Your face and turn from anything that is not of You. I pray You come and heal the land. In Jesus' name, Amen.

Meditate on 2 Chronicles 7:14

> If my people, who belong to me, humble themselves, pray, seek to please me, and repudiate their sinful practices, then I will respond from heaven, forgive their sin, and heal their land.

Write in your Faith Journal the words *humble, pray, seek* and *turn*. Reflect on each word. Write out what areas of your life you can apply and put these words into action.

Shade 37

"IF" is such a little word but it has a huge impact. YOU must choose to take action...even if you crawl. Move toward God...He promises to meet you.

Meditate on John 14:15-24

"If you love me, you will obey my commandments. Then I will ask the Father, and he will give you another Advocate to be with you forever— the Spirit of truth, whom the world cannot accept, because it does not see him or know him. But you know him, because he resides with you and will be in you. I will not abandon you as orphans, I will come to you. In a little while the world will not see me any longer, but you will see me; because I live, you will live too. You will know at that time that I am in my Father and you are in me and I am in you. The person who has my commandments and obeys them is the one who loves me. The one who loves me will be loved by my Father, and I will love him and will reveal myself to him." "Lord," Judas (not Judas Iscariot) said, "What has happened that you are going to reveal yourself to us and not to the world?" Jesus replied, "If anyone loves me, he will obey my word, and my Father will love him, and we will come to him and take up residence with him. The person who does not love me does not obey my words. And the

word you hear is not mine, but the Father's who sent me.

Write in your Faith Journal all the amazing blessings you have when you choose to love and obey Christ

Shade 38

"Who am I that you are mindful of me"? Have you ever wondered this? How God, who by only His Word, created everything out of nothing, thinks of you? How can the "everything" God care for, desire, delight, listen to and love you? Well...HE does! And His very Word is holding you now. Yes, He is mindful of you. He knows exactly where you are. He sees your life and longs to be right in the middle of it. Seek Him! Find Him! He isn't hiding. He cares for you.

Meditate on Psalms 8:4 (KJV)
> *What is man, that thou art mindful of him? and the son of man, that thou visitest him?*

Write in your Faith Journal a prayer of thanksgiving to the "everything" God who sees you.

Shade 39

When Christ is your center you don't have to fight for position. Just be available to Him...He has already positioned you for greatness.

You were made to shine!

Meditate on Ephesians 1:3-8

> *Blessed is the God and Father of our Lord Jesus Christ, who has blessed us with every spiritual blessing in the heavenly realms in Christ. For he chose us in Christ before the foundation of the world that we may be holy and unblemished in his sight in love. He did this by predestining us to adoption as his sons through Jesus Christ, according to the pleasure of his will— to the praise of the glory of his grace that he has freely bestowed on us in his dearly loved Son. In him we have redemption through his blood, the forgiveness of our trespasses, according to the riches of his grace that he lavished on us in all wisdom and insight.*

Matthew 5:14-16

> *You are the light of the world. A city located on a hill cannot be hidden. People do not light a lamp and put it under a basket but on a lampstand, and it gives light to all in the house. In the same way, let your light shine before people, so that they can see your good deeds and give honor to your Father in heaven.*

Write in your Faith Journal how being "the Light" of the world can change those living in darkness.

Shade 40

In secret He created your fingerprint. It belongs only to you. That's how much God desires to be close to you. Evidence of Him is right at your fingertips. Place your fingertips from your left hand with the ones on your right hand, bow and speak...He can't wait to hear from you.

Blessings,

Meditate on Psalm 139:13-14
> *Certainly you made my mind and heart; you wove me together in my mother's womb. I will give you thanks because your deeds are awesome and amazing. You knew me thoroughly.*

Write in your Faith Journal a special time and place that you can meet with the Father for one-on-one time with Him.

Shade 41

No matter your "storm" God says "It's handled...TRUST ME." As sure as you grab that umbrella when it's raining to keep you from getting wet, you should have the same assurance that God won't let you sink. Keep your eyes on Christ and you will make it through to the other side.

Meditate on Psalms 107:29

> *He calmed the storm, and the waves grew silent.*

Write in your Faith Journal what it means to you that Christ can hush any storm in your life. If you find yourself in the middle of a storm right now...pray...be still...know that Jesus is right in the middle of it.

Shade 42

Even when the sun isn't shining, it's still there. Even when you can't see the SON, HE is ALWAYS watching. Jesus is always watching over you. He calls you His very own. He has counted every hair on your head. You are His and, just like earthly parents, He is very protective of you. He will not let you fail. In His name nothing can come against you. NOTHING. He loves you with a love that is overflowing and overwhelming. In the darkest of night, in the darkest of times...you are never hidden from Him.

Meditate on Joshua 1:9

> *I repeat, be strong and brave! Don't be afraid and don't panic, for I, the Lord your God, am with you in all you do.*

Write in your Faith Journal about a time you experienced the presence of God when you didn't believe He saw your circumstance.

Shade 43

There are moments in the day I reflect on my life and am overcome with thankfulness! God has NEVER failed me. I may have failed Him at times but HE has covered each failure with love and wisdom. With every tear, every smile, every pain, every joy...HE has been there...before me, beside me, carrying me. I am in awe of His lovingkindness and it brings me to my knees! If you don't KNOW Him... open your eyes and SEE. The trees stand in honor of Him. The mountains declare His glory and the Earth spins at the tip of His finger. He has it all under His divine control. Without Him, there is chaos. With Him all things are in order. Let Him into your life and see what He does in and through your life!

Meditate on Psalm 63:3
Because experiencing your loyal love is better than life itself, my lips will praise you.

Write in your Faith Journal a song of praise to the Lord. Put on your favorite worship song and praise Him for the great God He is.

Shade 44

Who do you think you are? You are Beloved, Apple of His eye, Redeemed, Rescued, Friend, Justified, No Longer Condemned, Chosen, Peaceful, Victorious, Seated in Heavenly places, Sealed, Alive, Made New, Blessed, Free, and a Joint Heir to The Kingdom!... That's who YOU are!

Meditate of these scriptures:

1 John 3:3

>And everyone who has this hope focused on him purifies himself, just as Jesus is pure.

Ephesians 1:6

>To the praise of the glory of his grace that he has freely bestowed on us in his dearly loved Son.

John 1:12

>But to all who have received him—those who believe in his name—he has given the right to become God's children.

Rom. 8:17

>And if children, then heirs (namely, heirs of God and also fellow heirs with Christ)—if indeed we suffer with him so we may also be glorified with him.

Colossians 1:14

>In whom we have redemption, the forgiveness of sins.

2 Corinthians 1:21

>But it is God who establishes us together with you in Christ and who anointed us.

Write in your Faith Journal WHO YOU ARE.

Shade 45

We all want a "soulmate" but the only one fit for our soul is JESUS CHRIST! Fall in love with Him. He will fill your life with EVERYTHING you need for it to be abundant! Jesus, Lover of My Soul!

Meditate on Psalm 103:2-5

> Praise the Lord, O my soul! Do not forget all his kind deeds! He is the one who forgives all your sins, who heals all your diseases, who delivers your life from the Pit, who crowns you with his loyal love and compassion, who satisfies your life with good things, so your youth is renewed like an eagle's.

Write in your Faith Journal what it means to have Jesus Christ as your soulmate.

Shade 46

To someone swallowed up in darkness, you may be their only encounter with LIGHT! We are called to make Him known! Be grace, mercy, peace, hope, kindness and love to everyone.

Meditate on 1 Corinthians 11:1

> Be imitators of me, just as I also am of Christ.

Write in your Faith Journal the reflection you see when you look in the mirror. Are you reflecting Christ or the world?

Shade 47

My Father is the greatest artist ever! I'm so in awe of Him! He can paint the sky and still...we are always on His mind! I'm so wrapped up in His love! You are too! It's going to be a GREAT DAY!

Meditate on Isaiah 66:2
> My hand made them; that is how they came to be," says the Lord. I show special favor to the humble and contrite, who respect what I have to say.

Write in your Faith Journal how you believe the love of God is evident in creation.

Shade 48

Who or what has your full attention? Who or what are you listening to? Do you know His voice?

Meditate on Luke 19:48
> But they could not find a way to do it, for all the people hung on his words.

Write in your Faith Journal some of the influences in your life. Are they of Christ? Is He your greatest influence? How can you guard your heart, mind and life?

Shade 49

When it's hard to have joy in the hurt, hardships, loneliness, sickness and brokenness of this life, REJOICE in who God is in the midst of it all!

Meditate on Philippians 4:4
> *Rejoice in the Lord always. Again I say, rejoice!*

Write in your Faith Journal why you believe it is important to have joy in all situations.

Shade 50

Nothing will ever prepare your heart to see your child struggling with addiction. It's the ugliest thing on earth. I've heard, "Ok Mom, tomorrow I'll go," for 8 years. Something that fits into the palm of a hand controls an entire being. But I am in the hands of the Ruler of the Universe. He heals the brokenhearted and makes the impossible possible. I'll keep praying for the possible and keep hope in each tomorrow, for TODAY is a NEW day, a NEW chance...a first step!

When life knocks you down into the dirt remember you are a seed. Grow through it! Reach out and help others. Spread the good seeds of Christ and one by one we will be the Light of this world.

Faith Journal

Shade 1

Mediate on Psalm 95:6:

> Come! Let's bow down and worship! Let's kneel before the LORD, our creator!

What did you experience from bowing down before Him?

_____

_____

_____

_____

_____

Shade 2

Meditate on Hebrews 4:12:

> For the word of God is living and active and sharper than any double-edged sword, piercing even to the point of dividing soul from spirit, and joints from marrow; it is able to judge the desires and thoughts of the heart.

Write in your Faith Journal what new things were revealed about God in your "appointment" with Him.

_____

_____

_____

_____

_____

Shade 3

Meditate on Isaiah 65:5:

> *They say, 'Keep to yourself! Don't get near me, for I am holier than you!' These people are like smoke in my nostrils, like a fire that keeps burning all day long.*

Write in your Faith Journal how you may have an attitude of "holier than thou" and how you plan to change it.

_____

_____

_____

_____

_____

Shade 4

Meditate on Proverbs 25:21-22:

> *If your enemy is hungry, give him food to eat, and if he is thirsty, give him water to drink, for*

you will heap coals of fire on his head, and the Lord will reward you.

Write in your Faith Journal ways you can be the Love and Light of Christ to others.

_____

_____

_____

_____

_____

Shade 5

Meditate on Romans 5:8:
> *But God demonstrates his own love for us, in that while we were still sinners, Christ died for us.*

Write in your Faith Journal some of the ways you have felt His love today.

_____

_____

_____

_____

_____

Shade 6

Meditate on this scripture: Hebrews 13:8:

> *Jesus Christ is the same yesterday and today and forever!*

Write in your Faith Journal what knowing this truth means to you

_____

_____

_____

_____

_____

Shade 7

Meditate on Ephesians 2:4-5:

> *But God, being rich in mercy, because of his great love with which he loved us, even though we were dead in transgressions, made us alive together with Christ—by grace you are saved!*

Write in your Faith Journal how this will help you in your walk with Christ.

_____

_____

_____

_____

_____

Shade 8

Meditate on Song of Solomon 2:16:
> *My lover is mine and I am his; he grazes among the lilies.*

Write in your Faith Journal what it means to belong to Him.

_____

_____

_____

_____

Shade 9

Meditate on 1 Corinthians 14:33:
> *For God is not characterized by disorder but by peace. As in all the churches of the saints,*

Write in your Faith Journal how meditating on this scripture helped you throughout your day.

_____

_____

_____

_____

_____

Shade 10

Meditate on Proverbs 18:21:

> *Death and life are in the power of the tongue,*
> *and those who love its use will eat its fruit.*

Write in your Faith Journal how this scripture has challenged you to become aware of your words.

_____

_____

_____

_____

_____

Shade 11

Meditate on Ephesians 1:4:

> *For he chose us in Christ before the foundation*
> *of the world that we may be holy and*
> *unblemished in his sight in love.*

Write in your Faith Journal what the word "chosen" means to you in light of this scripture.

_____

_____

_____

_____

_____

Shade 12

Meditate on Psalm 139:14 (NIV)

> *I praise you because I am fearfully and wonderfully made; your works are wonderful, I know that full well.*

Write in your Faith Journal what this scripture has meant to you today.

_____

_____

_____

_____

_____

Shade 13

Meditate on Ephesians 3:17-18

> *So that Christ may dwell in your hearts through faith. And I pray that you, being rooted and established in love, may have power, together with all the Lord's holy people, to grasp how wide and long and high and deep is the love of Christ.*

Write in your Faith Journal what this scripture has spoken to your heart today.

_____

_____

_____

_____

_____

Shade 14

Meditate on Isaiah 48:17 (NIV)

> *This is what the LORD says-- your Redeemer, the Holy One of Israel: "I am the LORD your God, who teaches you what is best for you, who directs you in the way you should go.*

Write in Your Faith Journal how you can let go and let God.

_____

_____

_____

_____

_____

Shade 15

Meditate on Revelation 3:20

> *Listen! I am standing at the door and knocking! If anyone hears my voice and opens the door I will come into his home and share a meal with him, and he with me.*

Romans 14:11

For it is written, "As I live, says the Lord, every knee will bow to me, and every tongue will give praise to God."

Write in Your Faith Journal what things may be preventing you from allowing Christ to be the Lord of your life.

_____

_____

_____

_____

Shade 16

Meditate on 1 John 4:4
> *You are from God, little children, and have conquered them, because the one who is in you is greater than the one who is in the world.*

Write in your Faith Journal about a time when God revealed Himself great in a situation in your life. He is still that same God.

_____

_____

_____

_____

Shade 17

Meditate on Ephesians 4:1-16
> *I, therefore, the prisoner for the Lord, urge you to live worthily of the calling with which you have been called, with all humility and gentleness, with patience, bearing with one another in love, making every effort to keep the unity of the Spirit in the bond of peace. There is one body and one Spirit, just as you too were called to the one hope of your calling, one Lord, one faith, one baptism, one God and*

Father of all, who is over all and through all and in all. But to each one of us grace was given according to the measure of the gift of Christ. Therefore it says, "When he ascended on high he captured captives; he gave gifts to men." Now what is the meaning of "he ascended," except that he also descended to the lower regions, namely, the earth? He, the very one who descended, is also the one who ascended above all the heavens, in order to fill all things. It was he who gave some as apostles, some as prophets, some as evangelists, and some as pastors and teachers, to equip the saints for the work of ministry, that is, to build up the body of Christ, until we all attain to the unity of the faith and of the knowledge of the Son of God—a mature person, attaining to the measure of Christ's full stature. So we are no longer to be children, tossed back and forth by waves and carried about by every wind of teaching by the trickery of people who craftily carry out their deceitful schemes. But practicing the truth in love, we will in all things grow up into Christ, who is the head. From him the whole body grows, fitted and held together through every supporting ligament. As each one does its part, the body grows in love.

Write in your Faith Journal how you plan to be active in a love that seeks the best for others.

_____

_____

_____

_____

_____

Shade 18

Proverbs 16:24
> *Pleasant words are like a honeycomb, sweet to the soul and healing to the bones.*

Write in your Faith Journal how a sweet word of encouragement helped you in the past.

_____

_____

_____

_____

Shade 19

Meditate on Colossians 1:27
> *God wanted to make known to them the glorious riches of this mystery among the*

Gentiles, which is Christ in you, the hope of glory.

Write in your Faith Journal how it feels to know that you will be with Christ forever.

_____

_____

_____

_____

_____

Shade 20

Meditate on Matthew 17:20

He told them, "It was because of your little faith. I tell you the truth, if you have faith the size of a mustard seed, you will say to this mountain, 'Move from here to there,' and it will move; nothing will be impossible for you."

Write in your Faith Journal a time when you thought a situation was impossible and God made it possible. Looking back now, should you doubt Him?

_____

_____

_____

Shade 21

Meditate on Galatians 5:22

But the fruit of the Spirit is love, joy, peace, patience, kindness, goodness, faithfulness,

Jeremiah 1:5

Before I formed you in your mother's womb I chose you. Before you were born I set you apart. I appointed you to be a prophet to the nations.

Write in your Faith Journal how you feel knowing HE had a plan for your life and watches over you and that plan which He placed in you since the beginning of time.

_____

_____

_____

_____

_____

Shade 22

Meditate on 2 Corinthians 5:17

> *So then, if anyone is in Christ, he is a new creation; what is old has passed away—look, what is new has come!*

Write in your Faith Journal some things that you have not reconciled. Pray over them. Do not allow them room any longer. If you need to forgive or be forgiven, settle it today and now that God makes it all new and you no longer have to live in the bondage of the old.

_____

_____

_____

_____

_____

Shade 23

Meditate on Romans 10:13:

> *For everyone who calls on the name of the Lord will be saved.*

Write in your Faith Journal someone you know that has not accepted the free gift of Salvation and commit to praying for them and being the light in this dark world that leads them to His Grace.

_____

_____

_____

_____

_____

Shade 24

Meditate on Psalm 1:1-3:

> *How blessed is the one who does not follow the advice of the wicked, or stand in the pathway with sinners, or sit in the assembly of scoffers! Instead he finds pleasure in obeying the Lord's commands; he meditates on his commands day and night. He is like a tree planted by flowing streams; it yields its fruit at the proper time, and its leaves never fall off. He succeeds in everything he attempts.*

Write in your Faith Journal a time when you were "religious" in thinking and how it affected your life. Then write about a time when you were living in "relationship" with Christ and how it affected you.

_____

_____

_____

_____

_____

Shade 25

Meditate on Isaiah 43:18-19:

> *Don't remember these earlier events; don't recall these former events. Look, I am about to do something new. Now it begins to happen! Do you not recognize it? Yes, I will make a road in the desert and paths in the wilderness.*

Write in your Faith Journal ways you can move forward and stop answering the door to the past.

_____

_____

_____

_____

Shade 26

Meditate on Psalm 136:26:

> *Give thanks to the God of heaven, for his loyal love endures!*

Write in your Faith Journal some of the names of God and spend time worshipping Him, thanking Him, giving honor to only Him.

Shade 27

Meditate on Jeremiah 29:11:

> For I know what I have planned for you,' says the Lord. 'I have plans to prosper you, not to harm you. I have plans to give you a future filled with hope.

Write in your Faith Journal something you know God has called you to do but you have been afraid or you have put it off. Then make an action plan to get it done, knowing He has already given you the tools to succeed.

_____

_____

Shade 28

Meditate on Hebrews 1:3-4:

> *The Son is the radiance of his glory and the representation of his essence, and he sustains all things by his powerful word, and so when he had accomplished cleansing for sins, he sat down at the right hand of the Majesty on high. Thus he became so far better than the angels as he has inherited a name superior to theirs.*

Write in your Faith Journal how you ARE going to trust God with the situations in your life and become free of the chains as you link your heart and hope to Christ who is seated at the right hand of God.

_____

_____

_____

_____

_____

Shade 29

Meditate on Philippians 4:8:

> *Finally, brothers and sisters, whatever is true, whatever is worthy of respect, whatever is just, whatever is pure, whatever is lovely, whatever is commendable, if something is excellent or praiseworthy, think about these things.*

Write in your Faith Journal some of the good, pure, lovely, true, just, virtuous and praiseworthy things in your life.

_____

_____

_____

_____

_____

Shade 30

Meditate on 1 John 2:3-6

> *Now by this we know that we have come to know God: if we keep his commandments. The one who says "I have come to know God" and yet does not keep his commandments is a liar, and the truth is not in such a person. But whoever obeys his word, truly in this person the love of God has been perfected. By this we know that we are in him. The one who says he*

resides in God ought himself to walk just as Jesus walked.

Write in your Faith Journal what you KNOW to be true about God and ways you can get to know Him better.

_____

_____

_____

_____

_____

Shade 31

Meditate on 1 Peter 5:7:

> *And God will exalt you in due time, if you humble yourselves under his mighty hand by casting all your cares on him because he cares for you.*

Write in your Faith Journal how you will decide to turn all your concerns over to Him and leave them there.

_____

_____

_____

_____

Shade 32

Meditate on Romans 15:13:

> *Now may the God of hope fill you with all joy and peace as you believe in him, so that you may abound in hope by the power of the Holy Spirit.*

Galatians 4:6

> *And because you are sons, God sent the Spirit of his Son into our hearts, who calls "Abba! Father!"*

Write in your Faith Journal what it means to you to have "ABBA FATHER" as your guardian.

_____

_____

_____

_____

_____

Shade 33

Meditate on 2 Thessalonians 3:3:
> *But the Lord is faithful, and he will strengthen you and protect you from the evil one.*

Write in your Faith Journal how God was faithful, even when you were not so faithful.

_____

_____

_____

_____

_____

Shade 34

Meditate on Isaiah 41:10:
> *Don't be afraid, for I am with you! Don't be frightened, for I am your God! I strengthen you—yes, I help you—yes, I uphold you with my saving right hand!*

Write in your Faith Journal how you are going to overcome the fear in your life and get unstuck.

_____

_____

_____

Shade 35

Meditate on Isaiah 30:19
> *For people will live in Zion; in Jerusalem you will weep no more. When he hears your cry of despair, he will indeed show you mercy; when he hears it, he will respond to you.*

Write in your Prayer Journal an answer to prayer that was nothing like you expected.

_____

_____

_____

_____

_____

Shade 36

Meditate on 2 Chronicles 7:14
> *If my people, who belong to me, humble themselves, pray, seek to please me, and repudiate their sinful practices, then I will respond from heaven, forgive their sin, and heal their land.*

Write in your Faith Journal the words *humble, pray, seek* and *turn.* Reflect on each word. Write out what areas of your life you can apply and put these words into action.

_____

_____

_____

_____

_____

Shade 37

Meditate on John 14:15-24

"If you love me, you will obey my commandments. Then I will ask the Father, and he will give you another Advocate to be with you forever— the Spirit of truth, whom the world cannot accept, because it does not see him or know him. But you know him, because he resides with you and will be in you. I will not abandon you as orphans, I will come to you. In a little while the world will not see me any longer, but you will see me; because I live, you will live too. You will know at that time that I am in my Father and you are in me and I am in you. The person who has my commandments and obeys them is the one who loves me. The one who loves me will be

loved by my Father, and I will love him and will reveal myself to him." "Lord," Judas (not Judas Iscariot) said, "What has happened that you are going to reveal yourself to us and not to the world?" Jesus replied, "If anyone loves me, he will obey my word, and my Father will love him, and we will come to him and take up residence with him. The person who does not love me does not obey my words. And the word you hear is not mine, but the Father's who sent me.

Write in your Faith Journal all the amazing blessings you have when you choose to love and obey Christ

_____

_____

_____

_____

_____

Shade 38

Meditate on Psalms 8:4 (KJV)
What is man, that thou art mindful of him? and the son of man, that thou visitest him?

Write in your Faith Journal a prayer of thanksgiving to the everything God who sees you.

_____

_____

_____

_____

_____

Shade 39

Meditate on Ephesians 1:3-8

> *Blessed is the God and Father of our Lord Jesus Christ, who has blessed us with every spiritual blessing in the heavenly realms in Christ. For he chose us in Christ before the foundation of the world that we may be holy and unblemished in his sight in love. He did this by predestining us to adoption as his sons through Jesus Christ, according to the pleasure of his will— to the praise of the glory of his grace that he has freely bestowed on us in his dearly loved Son. In him we have redemption through his blood, the forgiveness of our trespasses, according to the riches of his grace that he lavished on us in all wisdom and insight.*

Matthew 5:14-16

> *You are the light of the world. A city located on a hill cannot be hidden. People do not light a lamp and put it under a basket but on a lampstand, and it gives light to all in the*

house. In the same way, let your light shine before people, so that they can see your good deeds and give honor to your Father in heaven.

Write in your Faith Journal how being "the Light" of the world can change those living in darkness.

_____

_____

_____

_____

_____

Shade 40

Meditate on Psalm 139:13-14

Certainly you made my mind and heart; you wove me together in my mother's womb. I will give you thanks because your deeds are awesome and amazing. You knew me thoroughly.

Write in your Faith Journal a special time and place that you can meet with the Father for one-on-one time with Him.

_____

_____

_____

_____

_____

Shade 41

Meditate on Psalms 107:29
> *He calmed the storm, and the waves grew silent.*

Write in your Faith Journal what it means to you that Christ can hush any storm in your life. If you find yourself in the middle of a storm right now...pray...be still...know that Jesus is right in the middle of it.

_____

_____

_____

_____

_____

Shade 42

Meditate on Joshua 1:9
> *I repeat, be strong and brave! Don't be afraid and don't panic, for I, the Lord your God, am with you in all you do.*

Write in your Faith Journal about a time you experienced the presence of God when you didn't believe He saw your circumstance.

_____

_____

_____

_____

_____

Shade 43

Meditate on Psalm 63:3

> *Because experiencing your loyal love is better than life itself, my lips will praise you.*

Write in your Faith Journal a song of praise to the Lord. Put on your favorite worship song and praise Him for the great God He is.

_____

_____

_____

_____

_____

Shade 44

Meditate of these scriptures:

1 John 3:3
> *And everyone who has this hope focused on him purifies himself, just as Jesus is pure.*

Ephesians 1:6
> *To the praise of the glory of his grace that he has freely bestowed on us in his dearly loved Son.*

John 1:12
> *But to all who have received him—those who believe in his name—he has given the right to become God's children.*

Romnas 8:17
> *And if children, then heirs (namely, heirs of God and also fellow heirs with Christ)—if indeed we suffer with him so we may also be glorified with him.*

Colossians 1:14
> *In whom we have redemption, the forgiveness of sins.*

2 Corinthians 1:21
> *But it is God who establishes us together with you in Christ and who anointed us.*

Write in your Faith Journal WHO YOU ARE.

_____

_____

_____

_____

_____

Shade 45

Meditate on Psalm 103:2-5

> *Praise the Lord, O my soul! Do not forget all his kind deeds! He is the one who forgives all your sins, who heals all your diseases, who delivers your life from the Pit, who crowns you with his loyal love and compassion, who satisfies your life with good things, so your youth is renewed like an eagle's.*

Write in your Faith Journal what it means to have Jesus Christ as your soulmate.

_____

_____

_____

_____

_____

Shade 46

Meditate on 1 Corinthians 11:1
> *Be imitators of me, just as I also am of Christ.*

Write in your Faith Journal the reflection you see when you look in the mirror. Are you reflecting Christ or the world?

_____

_____

_____

_____

_____

Shade 47

Meditate on Isaiah 66:2
> *My hand made them; that is how they came to be," says the Lord. I show special favor to the humble and contrite, who respect what I have to say.*

Write in your Faith Journal how you believe the love of God is evident in creation.

_____

_____

_____

Shade 48

Meditate on Luke 19:48
> *But they could not find a way to do it, for all the people hung on his words.*

Write in your Faith Journal some of the influences in your life. Are they of Christ? Is He your greatest influence? How can you guard your heart, mind and life?

_____

_____

_____

_____

_____

Shade 49

Meditate on Philippians 4:4
> *Rejoice in the Lord always. Again I say, rejoice!*

Write in your Faith Journal why you believe it is important to have joy in all situations.

_____

_____

_____

_____

_____

Shade 50

What did you learn from these lessons?

_____

_____

_____

_____

_____

Other Books by Heart Thoughts Publishing

Visit us at **www.HeartThoughtsPublishing.com**
Or email us at
Info@HeartThoughtsPublishing.com

Made in the USA
Lexington, KY
16 April 2017